NASCAR RACING

NASCAR's Wildest Wrecks

by Matt Doeden

Consultant:
Betty L. Carlan
Research Librarian
International Motorsports Hall of Fame
Talladega, Alabama

Capstone Press

Mankato, Minnesota

Edge Books are published by Capstone Press,
151 Good Counsel Drive, P.O. Box 669, Mankato, Minnesota 56002.
www.capstonepress.com

Library of Congress Cataloging-in-Publication Data
Doeden, Matt.
    NASCAR's wildest wrecks / by Matt Doeden.
    p. cm.—(Edge Books. NASCAR racing)
    Includes bibliographical references and index.
    ISBN 0-7368-3775-2 (hardcover)
    ISBN 0-7368-5234-4 (paperback)
    1. Stock car racing—United States—Accidents—Juvenile literature. 2. Stock car
racing—United States—Safety measures—Juvenile literature. 3. NASCAR (Association)—
Juvenile literature. I. Title. II. Series.
GV1029.9.S74D64 2005
796.72—dc22
                                                2004012364

Summary: Discusses famous NASCAR crashes and the safety innovations that were
    implemented because of them.

Editorial Credits
Tom Adamson, editor; Jason Knudson, set designer; Enoch Peterson, book designer;
    Jo Miller, photo researcher; Scott Thoms, photo editor

Photo Credits
AP/Wide World Photos/Russell Williams, 15; Jim Topper, 17; Kevin Rivoli, 26
Corbis/Reuters, 5, 6, 7, 28; NewSport/George Tiedemann, 8; Sam Sharpe, 23
Getty Images Inc./Robert Laberge, cover; Rusty Jarrett, 12
Navy Photo/PHC Edward G. Martens, 24
Sam Sharpe, 13, 14, 25
SportsChrome Inc./Greg Crisp, 11; Brian Spurlock, 18

1 2 3 4 5 6 10 09 08 07 06 05

Table of Contents

Chapter 1:
Ryan Newman's Wild Ride 4

Chapter 2:
Causing a Wreck 10

Chapter 3:
Famous Wrecks 16

Chapter 4:
Learning from Wrecks 22

The Pass in the Grass 21

Glossary 30

Read More 31

Internet Sites 31

Index 32

Ryan Newman's Wild Ride

Ryan Newman started the 2003 Daytona 500 near the back. But he had a good car. He began passing other drivers, moving up to 15th place by lap 57.

Newman and Ken Schrader were speeding side by side down the frontstretch. Ward Burton tapped the left rear of Schrader's car. The contact was light. Still, at about 190 miles (306 kilometers) per hour, it caused Schrader to lose control of his car. Schrader bounced off the wall and slammed into Newman's Dodge.

Newman gripped the steering wheel and tried to keep the car from spinning. But he had no chance. His tires had already started to slide.

Ryan Newman's car tore up dirt and grass as it hit the infield.

Learn about:

→ Rollover wreck

→ Destroyed race car

→ Roll cages

5

Newman's car slid up the track. The car bounced off the wall and back down the track toward the grassy infield.

Newman's car flipped as it hit the grass. The rear axle snapped, sending small parts flying everywhere. Even the wheels flew off. The car rolled over four times. It finally landed on its roof and slid to a stop.

Newman's car rolled over four times during the wreck.

Countless pieces of the race car flew off during the rollover.

Newman was trapped upside down in the car. A huge pile of grass and dirt pinned him inside. Rescue crews rushed to help him out of the car.

Safety

Newman's crash looked bad. His car was completely destroyed. But Newman was not seriously hurt. The car's roll cage kept him safe.

Rescue workers hurried to get Newman out of the wrecked car.

All race cars have roll cages. This system of strong metal tubes surrounds the driver. In a rollover or collision, the driver is protected inside that cage. Newman was racing again the next week.

Each car has many safety features to protect drivers during flips, spins, and collisions. NASCAR teams do everything they can to help drivers walk away from even the biggest wrecks.

"I had a wad of sod about 8 inches thick and 2 feet long sitting in my lap and I couldn't get out of the car."
—Ryan Newman, News-Journal Online, 2-17-03

CHAPTER 2

Causing a Wreck

Almost every NASCAR race includes at least one wreck. Drivers often argue about who started a wreck, but most wrecks have one of a few basic causes.

Stock Car Handling

A stock car's handling is one of its most important features. A good car drives through turns smoothly. But cars rarely handle perfectly.

Stock cars are tight when they don't turn easily. Drivers with tight cars can't enter turns at top speed. They have to crank the steering wheel hard just to get through the turns.

A loose car is the opposite of a tight car. A loose car's rear tires can lose their grip. When the driver turns the steering wheel, the rear of the car slides, or fishtails. A loose car often wiggles as it enters or exits a turn. This wiggle can cause the car to spin out or brush the wall.

Learn about:

→ Handling

→ Equipment failure

→ Restrictor plate racing

Tires and Engines

Some wrecks happen when a car has a blown tire or engine failure. These equipment failures can cause a car to slow down suddenly. Other drivers might crash while trying to avoid the slowing car.

A tire could go flat at any time. A driver might run over something on the track, resulting in a cut tire. A cut tire often blows up

A cut tire can even take a driver out of the race.

Engine failures can cause wrecks.

without warning. If the car is in a turn, it will usually slam into the wall.

Blown engines can also cause wrecks. Cars can easily pile up behind a car with a blown engine. Many engine failures cause oil to leak onto the track. Other drivers who hit this oil can suddenly lose control of their cars.

Restrictor plates cause cars to bunch together in tight packs.

Restrictor Plates

During the late 1980s, stock cars were becoming more powerful. They could reach speeds that were too dangerous even for racing. Daytona and Talladega were the fastest tracks. Crashes at these tracks were especially dangerous to drivers and fans because of the high speeds.

NASCAR changed the rules to slow down the cars at these tracks. Teams had to add restrictor plates to their engines. These metal plates prevent air from entering the engine.

Without enough air, the engines can't burn fuel as quickly. The cars then don't race as fast.

Restrictor plates have another effect on races. They make drafting important. Cars need to follow closely behind other cars to reduce air resistance. The engines don't have enough power to keep up unless the driver stays in the draft.

Because of drafting, cars with restrictor plates usually run very close together in large groups. If one driver makes a small mistake, a dozen or more cars can crash. Ryan Newman's crash at Daytona in 2003 happened because the cars raced so closely together.

With just one small mistake, several cars can get caught up in a wreck.

CHAPTER 3

Famous Wrecks

The 2001 NASCAR season began with one of the worst days of wrecks in racing history. The first wreck looked terrible, but no one was hurt. Another wreck that day changed NASCAR forever.

The 2001 Daytona 500

With about 25 laps remaining in the 2001 Daytona 500, Robby Gordon bumped Ward Burton. Burton slowed down to regain control of his car. Behind him, other drivers tried to slow down and move out of his way. But the cars were running too close together.

Tony Stewart lost control of his Pontiac. The car flew into the air. Stewart's car bounced off another car and flipped several times. The car landed on top of Bobby Labonte's car.

The wreck included 18 cars. As bad as the wreck looked, no driver had any major injuries.

Tony Stewart (#20) was not seriously injured after this frightening wreck.

Learn about:

→ Tragedy at Daytona

→ Waltrip at Bristol

→ Injured fans

Dale Earnhardt, NASCAR's most famous driver, died in a wreck in 2001.

> "I don't know what happened—all of a sudden we were all crashing . . . We hit pretty hard and Dale hit harder."
>
> —Ken Schrader, nascar.com, 2-21-01

On the last lap, Dale Earnhardt and Sterling Marlin were racing for third place. In the final turn, they made contact. Earnhardt's car spun. Ken Schrader ran into him, and Earnhardt smashed into the outside wall.

Many fans didn't notice the crash right away. They were watching Michael Waltrip win the race. Soon, everyone noticed that Earnhardt had not left his car. Emergency crews rushed to help him. But Earnhardt had died instantly in the crash.

Waltrip's Wreck

Not all of NASCAR's worst wrecks happen during a race. Some crashes happen during qualifying. During qualifying, drivers go as fast as they can for two laps to earn a spot in the race.

In April 1990, Michael Waltrip was qualifying for a race at Bristol. He lost control of his car and slammed into a gate. The gate cut Waltrip's car almost in half. Waltrip walked away from the crash without serious injury.

Bobby Allison's Wreck

In 1987, Bobby Allison was racing with the lead pack in the Winston 500 at Talladega. Allison was going more than 200 miles (320 kilometers) per hour as he entered the turn along the frontstretch.

Suddenly, one of Allison's tires blew up. His car shot up the track and into the air. It slammed into a metal fence. Hundreds of pieces broke off the car.

Many pieces flew into the stands. Several fans were injured. One man lost his sight in one eye after being struck by a piece of the car.

Even though Allison stayed safe, many fans could have been killed. Allison's crash convinced NASCAR to add restrictor plates to the cars at Daytona and Talladega.

The Pass in the Grass

NASCAR drivers often save a car from what looks like a sure wreck. Dale Earnhardt's 1987 Pass in the Grass is one of the most famous saves in NASCAR history.

Earnhardt and Bill Elliott were racing for the lead in The Winston. With 10 laps left, they were bumping each other coming down the frontstretch. Elliott bumped Earnhardt onto the grassy infield. Everyone thought Earnhardt would spin out. But he kept control and accelerated through the grass. He moved back onto the track with the lead. Earnhardt saved his car from a wreck. He also won the race.

CHAPTER 4

Learning from Wrecks

NASCAR learns from wrecks and finds ways to make racing safer. Window nets prevent drivers' arms from going outside the car during a flip. Soft walls lessen the impact during crashes. Roof flaps pop up and slow down a car that is spinning. Drivers wear fireproof clothing.

Fire Protection

In 1964, most drivers wore fireproof suits. Fireball Roberts was allergic to the fireproof material. He wore a cotton uniform.

On the seventh lap of the World 600, Junior Johnson's and Ned Jarrett's cars touched. Roberts was behind them. He tried to steer out of the way, but he lost control of his car and spun.

Jarrett's car spun into the inside wall and caught fire. Roberts also spun toward the inside wall. He slammed into the wall and into Jarrett's car. Roberts' car flipped, and the fuel tank burst open. Fuel flowed into the car and caught fire.

Roof flaps are designed to keep a race car from flipping over when it spins out.

Learn about:

→ A tragic fire
→ Stuck throttles
→ Head And Neck Support

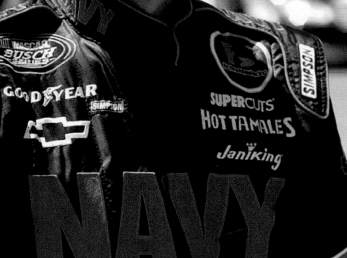

Drivers have to wear fireproof suits.

Jarrett ran to help Roberts. He pulled Roberts out by the shoulders. Rescue workers tried to get Roberts' burning suit off his body. By the time they pulled it off, Roberts was badly burned. He was rushed to the hospital. Roberts died several weeks later.

Roberts' crash, along with many others, led to some changes. Race cars now have fuel cells. Instead of a regular fuel tank, the fuel cell can withstand crashes. After the Roberts tragedy, NASCAR made all drivers wear fireproof clothing.

Fireproof clothing protects drivers during car fires.

The Kill Switch

In May 2000, Adam Petty was running practice laps at New Hampshire International Speedway. His throttle became stuck. He could not stop the engine and slow down the car. Petty brushed the wall, spun, then crashed hard into the wall. Rescue workers rushed Petty to the hospital, but he died of head injuries.

Some tracks have foam walls to protect drivers in head-on crashes.

Eight weeks later, Kenny Irwin was practicing at the same track. Irwin's throttle became stuck, and he smashed into the wall in almost the same spot Petty had. Irwin also died from his injuries.

After the deaths, NASCAR made teams add kill switches to the steering wheels of their cars. The kill switch is a button that instantly turns off the engine. A driver who feels the throttle sticking can hit the kill switch.

The HANS Device

Many of NASCAR's most serious injuries happen in head-on crashes. These crashes cause the driver's head and neck to snap forward quickly. Drivers can be killed or badly injured by this motion.

After Dale Earnhardt's 2001 crash, NASCAR decided every team needed to protect their drivers in these crashes. Today, drivers wear a Head And Neck Support (HANS).

Jim Downing helped invent the HANS device.

Shoulder straps attach the HANS to the driver's upper body. Straps connect it to the driver's helmet. The straps allow normal head movement but prevent the very fast motions that occur during head-on crashes.

Three months after Earnhardt's death, Ward Burton suffered a neck injury. His doctors agreed that without the HANS device, Burton would have broken his neck. The HANS device probably saved his life.

Stock car racing is a dangerous sport. No safety features can completely protect a driver. NASCAR teams keep working to make racing as safe as possible. Their work helps keep drivers safe in even the biggest wrecks.

"I don't think what makes a good race car driver is a fearless person. I think it's somebody that is comfortable being behind the wheel of something that's somewhat out of control."
—Jeff Gordon, 2-23-04

Glossary

axle (AK-suhl)—a rod in the center of a wheel, around which the wheel turns

drafting (DRAF-ting)—a strategy in which a driver closely follows another car to reduce air resistance

fishtail (FISH-tayl)—to have the rear end of a race car slide from side to side out of control

fuel cell (FYOO-uhl SELL)—the fuel tank in race cars; fuel cells are designed to withstand crashes.

HANS device (HANZ de-VISSE)—a system of straps that prevents the driver's head from snapping forward

restrictor plate (ri-STRIKT-ur PLAYT)—a device that limits the power of a race car's engine; the restrictor plate keeps down the car's speed for safety.

throttle (THROT-uhl)—a valve that controls the flow of fuel to the engine

Read More

Cavin, Curt. *Under the Helmet: Inside the Mind of a Driver.* The World of NASCAR. Chanhassen, Minn.: Tradition Books, 2004.

Johnstone, Michael. *NASCAR.* The Need for Speed. Minneapolis: LernerSports, 2002.

Schaefer, A. R. *The Daytona 500.* Edge Books NASCAR Racing. Mankato, Minn.: Capstone Press, 2004.

Woods, Bob. *Dirt Track Daredevils: The History of NASCAR.* The World of NASCAR. Excelsior, Minn.: Tradition Books, 2003.

Internet Sites

FactHound offers a safe, fun way to find Internet sites related to this book. All of the sites on FactHound have been researched by our staff.

Here's how:

1. Visit *www.facthound.com*
2. Type in this special code **0736837752** for age-appropriate sites. Or enter a search word related to this book for a more general search.
3. Click on the **Fetch It** button.

FactHound will fetch the best sites for you!

Index

Allison, Bobby, 20

Burton, Ward, 4, 16, 29

causes, 10, 12–15
clothing, 22, 25

Daytona 500, 4, 6–7, 16, 19
Daytona International
    Speedway, 14, 15, 20
drafting, 15

Earnhardt, Dale, 19, 21, 27
engines, 13, 14–15, 26, 27

fuel cells, 25

handling, 10
HANS device, 27, 29

Irwin, Kenny, 27

kill switches, 26–27

Newman, Ryan, 4, 6–9, 15

Petty, Adam, 26

restrictor plates, 14–15, 20
Roberts, Fireball, 22, 25
roll cage, 8–9
roof flaps, 22

Schrader, Ken, 4, 19
soft walls, 22
Stewart, Tony, 16

Talladega Superspeedway, 14,
    20
throttles, 26–27
tires, 10, 12–13, 20

Waltrip, Michael, 19, 20
window nets, 22